SandCastle™

Team Sports
By the Numbers

Baseball
By the Numbers

Mary Elizabeth Salzmann

Consulting Editor, Diane Craig, M.A./Reading Specialist

ABDO
Publishing Company

Published by ABDO Publishing Company, 8000 West 78th Street, Edina, Minnesota 55439.

Copyright © 2010 by Abdo Consulting Group, Inc. International copyrights reserved in all countries.

No part of this book may be reproduced in any form without written permission from the publisher. SandCastle™ is a trademark and logo of ABDO Publishing Company.

Printed in the United States.

 PRINTED ON RECYCLED PAPER

Editor: Katherine Hengel
Content Developer: Nancy Tuminelly
Cover and Interior Design and Production: Colleen Dolphin, Mighty Media
Photo Credits: iStockphoto (James Boulette), Shutterstock, Stockbyte

Library of Congress Cataloging-in-Publication Data

Salzmann, Mary Elizabeth, 1968-
  Baseball by the numbers / Mary Elizabeth Salzmann.
     p. cm. -- (Team sports by the numbers)
  ISBN 978-1-60453-767-3
  1. Baseball--Juvenile literature. 2. Arithmetic--Juvenile literature. I. Title.
  GV867.5.S25 2010
  796.357--dc22
                                    2009025789

SandCastle™ Level: Transitional

SandCastle™ books are created by a team of professional educators, reading specialists, and content developers around five essential components—phonemic awareness, phonics, vocabulary, text comprehension, and fluency—to assist young readers as they develop reading skills and strategies and increase their general knowledge. All books are written, reviewed, and leveled for guided reading, early reading intervention, and Accelerated Reader® programs for use in shared, guided, and independent reading and writing activities to support a balanced approach to literacy instruction. The SandCastle™ series has four levels that correspond to early literacy development. The levels are provided to help teachers and parents select appropriate books for young readers.

Emerging Readers
(no flags)

Beginning Readers
(1 flag)

Transitional Readers
(2 flags)

Fluent Readers
(3 flags)

SandCastle™ would like to hear from you. Please send us your comments and suggestions.
sandcastle@abdopublishing.com

Contents

Introduction.. 4

The Baseball Field 5

The Game.. 6

Offense.. 9

Defense 15

Baseball Facts 22

Answers to By the Numbers!........................ 23

Glossary.. 24

Introduction

Numbers are used all the time in baseball.

- A baseball **field** has 4 bases.

- The **pitcher's** mound is 10 inches (25.4 cm) high.

- A baseball game usually has 9 **innings**.

- Each team has to make 3 outs in an inning.

- After 3 **strikes**, a batter is out.

- After 4 balls, a batter gets a walk.

Let's learn more about how numbers are used in baseball.

The Baseball Field

60 feet, 6 inches
(18.4 m)

90 feet (27.4 m)

The Game

In baseball, there are 9 players on each team.

The teams take turns batting and **fielding**.

They **switch** when the fielding team gets 3 batters out.

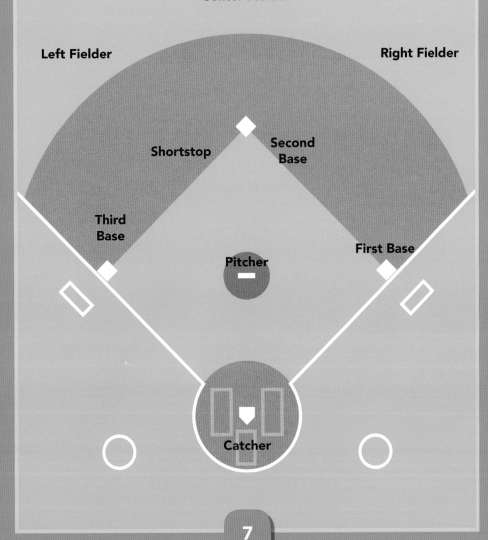

8

Offense

The team trying to score is the offense.

Jack is up to bat. He waits for the **pitch**.

By the Numbers!

A Jack can walk to first base if the pitcher throws 4 balls. The first 2 pitches were balls. How many more balls does Jack need to get a walk?

(answer on p. 23)

Tommy **slides** into third base.
He is safe!

By the Numbers!

B

To score a run, Tommy needs to touch all 4 bases.
He is on third base. How many more bases does
he have to touch?

(answer on p. 23)

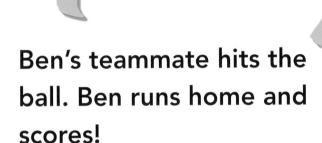

Ben's teammate hits the ball. Ben runs home and scores!

By the Numbers!

C

Ben's team already has 6 runs. How many will they have after Ben scores?

(answer on p. 23)

14

Defense

The team trying to keep the other team from scoring is the defense.

Emma is the **pitcher**. She tries to make the batter **strike** out.

By the Numbers!

D It takes 3 strikes for the batter to strike out. The batter has 1 strike. How many more strikes will it take for Emma to get the batter out?

(answer on p. 23)

Brandon is the catcher. He catches **pitches** that the batter doesn't hit.

By the Numbers!

E

So far Brandon has caught 3 balls and 2 **strikes**. How many total pitches has Brandon caught?

(answer on p. 23)

17

Connor catches a fly ball.
The batter is out!

By the Numbers!

F

There were already 2 outs. How many outs are there after Connor's catch?

(answer on p. 23)

Danny **fields** a ground ball. He will throw it to the first **baseman** to get the batter out.

By the Numbers!

G This will be the second out. After Danny's team gets 3 outs it will be their turn to bat. How many more outs do they need?

(answer on p. 23)

21

Baseball Facts

- The New York Yankees won the World Series 5 times in a row, from 1949 to 1953.

- In 1984 the Chicago White Sox and Milwaukee Brewers played a game that lasted 8 hours and 6 minutes.

- In 1920 the Brooklyn Dodgers and Boston Braves played a game that took 26 **innings**.

- Cal Ripken, Jr. played in 2,632 games in a row.

- **Pitcher** Nolan Ryan made 5,714 batters **strike** out.

- Ricky Henderson stole 1,406 bases.

- Pete Rose had 4,256 hits.

- Barry Bonds hit 73 home runs in 2001.

Answers to By the Numbers!

A

$$\begin{array}{r} 4 \\ -2 \\ \hline 2 \end{array}$$

Jack can walk to first base if the **pitcher** throws 4 balls. The first 2 pitches were balls. How many more balls does Jack need to get a walk?

B

$$\begin{array}{r} 4 \\ -3 \\ \hline 1 \end{array}$$

To score a run, Tommy needs to touch all 4 bases. He is on third base. How many more bases does he have to touch?

C

$$\begin{array}{r} 6 \\ +1 \\ \hline 7 \end{array}$$

Ben's team already has 6 runs. How many will they have after Ben scores?

D

$$\begin{array}{r} 3 \\ -1 \\ \hline 2 \end{array}$$

It takes 3 **strikes** for the batter to strike out. The batter has 1 strike. How many more strikes will it take for Emma to get the batter out?

E

$$\begin{array}{r} 3 \\ +2 \\ \hline 5 \end{array}$$

So far Brandon has caught 3 balls and 2 strikes. How many total pitches has Brandon caught?

F

$$\begin{array}{r} 2 \\ +1 \\ \hline 3 \end{array}$$

There were already 2 outs. How many outs are there after Connor's catch?

G

$$\begin{array}{r} 3 \\ -2 \\ \hline 1 \end{array}$$

This will be the second out. After Danny's team gets 3 outs it will be their turn to bat. How many more outs do they need?

Glossary

baseman – a player who covers the area around one of the bases.

field – 1. an outdoor area where a sport is played. 2. to be on the team trying to get the players on the batting team out. 3. to catch or pick up a ball after the batter hits it.

inning – one of the parts of a baseball game during which each team has a turn at bat. Most baseball games have nine innings.

pitch – a baseball thrown for a batter to hit. The *pitcher* is the player who throws the pitches.

slide – to dive headfirst or feet first to reach a base.

strike – a pitch that a batter misses or that is called a strike by the umpire.

switch – to change places or take turns.

To see a complete list of SandCastle™ books and other nonfiction titles
from ABDO Publishing Company, visit www.abdopublishing.com.
8000 West 78th Street, Edina, MN 55439 • 800-800-1312 • fax 952-831-1632